DATE DUE

Native American Chiefs
and Warriors

Oglala Sioux Chief
Crazy Horse

William R. Sanford

 Enslow Publishers, Inc.
40 Industrial Road
Box 398
Berkeley Heights, NJ 07922
USA

http://www.enslow.com

Original edition published as *Crazy Horse: Sioux Warrior* in 1994.

Library of Congress Cataloging-in-Publication Data

Sanford, William R. (William Reynolds), 1927-
Oglala Sioux Chief Crazy Horse / William R. Sanford.
  p. cm. — (Native American chiefs and warriors)
Includes bibliographical references and index.
ISBN 978-0-7660-4094-6
1. Crazy Horse, ca. 1842-1877—Juvenile literature. 2. Oglala Indians—Kings and rulers—Biography—Juvenile literature. 3. Little Bighorn, Battle of the, Mont., 1876—Juvenile literature. I. Title.
E99.O3C72915 2013
978.004'9752—dc23
[B]

                          2011048758

Future editions:

Paperback ISBN 978-1-4644-0261-6

ePUB ISBN 978-1-4645-1167-7

PDF ISBN 978-1-4646-1167-4

Printed in China

062012 Leo Paper Group, Heshan City, Guangdong, China

10 9 8 7 6 5 4 3 2 1

To Our Readers: We have done our best to make sure all Internet addresses in this book were active and appropriate when we went to press. However, the author and the publisher have no control over and assume no liability for the material available on those Internet sites or on other Web sites they may link to. Any comments or suggestions can be sent by e-mail to comments@enslow.com or to the address on the back cover.

Photo Credits: ©Clipart.com, pp. 6, 19; ©Corel Corporation, p. 16; Courtesy Little Bighorn Battlefield National Monument, p. 33; Library of Congress, pp. 8, 12, 21, 26, 28, 29, 37; ©2011 Photos.com, a division of Getty Images. All rights reserved. p. 17; Shutterstock.com, p. 41; Wikipedia, p. 24; William R. Sanford, p. 11, 32.

Cover Photo: Paul Daly

Contents

Author's Note 4

Chapter 1
On the Rosebud 5

Chapter 2
A Boy Called Curly 10

Chapter 3
The Warrior Crazy Horse 14

Chapter 4
The Fetterman Fight 18

Chapter 5
Red Cloud's War 23

Chapter 6
Crazy Horse Between Wars 27

Chapter 7
At the Little Bighorn 31

Chapter 8
Crazy Horse Surrenders 35

Chapter 9
The Killing of Crazy Horse 39

Chapter Notes 43

Glossary 45

Further Reading 46

Index 47

T his book tells the true story of the Oglala Sioux chief Crazy Horse. Many mistakenly believe that his fame rests on his defeat of the Seventh Cavalry. But his true fame comes from his leadership of the Oglala over many years. Following the Battle of the Little Bighorn, the press hurried to print stories about Crazy Horse. Some were made up, but others were true. The events described in this book all really happened.

Crazy Horse fought alongside other great Sioux leaders: Sitting Bull, Red Cloud, and Gall. Some believe Crazy Horse was the smartest and bravest of them all.

chapter 1

On the Rosebud

In mid June 1876, Crazy Horse camped on the Little Bighorn River in southern Montana. The war chief of the Oglala Sioux knew soldiers were coming close. His scouts watched their movements. A thousand soldiers were 30 miles to the south in the valley of Rosebud Creek. They wanted to drive the Sioux onto a reservation.

Two weeks earlier Crazy Horse had sent a warning to their leader General George Crook. "Every soldier who crosses the Tongue River will die."[1] Crazy Horse knew this prediction would come true. The Oglala medicine man, Sitting Bull, had a vision during a Sun Dance. He saw many soldiers falling into the Sioux camp. "I give you these because they have no ears," *Wakan Tanka* (the Great Holy) said.[2]

On June 16, Crazy Horse led 1,500 warriors toward the Rosebud Valley. On their flanks were *akicita*. These veteran warriors kept the young warriors in line. Crazy Horse did not want anyone dashing to the attack alone, thereby warning the soldiers.

After dawn on June 17, Crazy Horse stopped to apply war paint. He painted small white circles across his chest. Then he painted a streak of forked lightning across his cheek. Over one shoulder was a buckskin cord. On this cord was a little white stone with a hole in it. He fastened the skin of a red-backed hawk in his hair. Crazy Horse believed in his "medicine." It assured him he could not be harmed in battle.

Crazy Horse painted lightning and hail on his body before the Battle of Rosebud Creek. He would not let his photograph be taken, as he believed that by doing so his soul would be stolen.

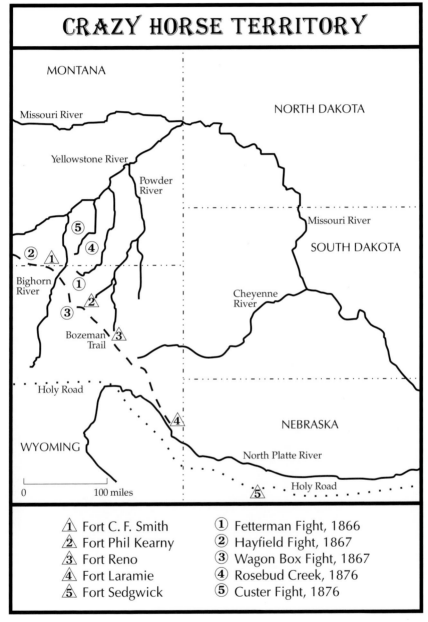

CRAZY HORSE TERRITORY

MONTANA

NORTH DAKOTA

Missouri River

Yellowstone River

Powder River

⑤

② Ⓐ①

Bighorn River

④

Missouri River

SOUTH DAKOTA

① Ⓐ②

③

Bozeman Trail

Ⓐ③

Cheyenne River

Holy Road

④

NEBRASKA

WYOMING

North Platte River

0   100 miles

Ⓐ⑤ · · Holy Road

Ⓐ1	Fort C. F. Smith	①	Fetterman Fight, 1866
Ⓐ2	Fort Phil Kearny	②	Hayfield Fight, 1867
Ⓐ3	Fort Reno	③	Wagon Box Fight, 1867
Ⓐ4	Fort Laramie	④	Rosebud Creek, 1876
Ⓐ5	Fort Sedgwick	⑤	Custer Fight, 1876

Crazy Horse led battles in Wyoming and Montana.

1

At 8:30 A.M. Crazy Horse resumed his march. About the same time General Crook stopped his troops to rest. Crook's force contained 201 infantry and 839 cavalry. Also with Crook were 262 Crow and Shoshoni scouts. Crazy Horse reached the Rosebud Valley. He hid his men behind a high hill. Then Crazy Horse crept to the top of a ridge. He saw Crook's forces scattered on both sides of the river. To the north the mile-long valley narrowed to a timbered canyon.

Almost at once Crow scouts spotted Crazy Horse. They rode toward Crook's camp, shouting, "Sioux! Sioux!"[3] The Sioux charged into the valley. Only the Crows and Shoshonis were ready to meet them. The rocky terrain prevented attacks in large groups. The battle became every man for himself.

This illustration shows General Crook's troops crossing the west fork of Goose Creek the day before the Battle of the Rosebud on July 18, 1876.

The Sioux charged the soldiers again and again. The firing lasted throughout the morning.

At one point, Jack Red Cloud lost his horse. The son of the famed Sioux chief Red Cloud had to run on foot. The Crows surrounded Jack Red Cloud. They ripped off his war bonnet and took his rifle. Crazy Horse saw this and spurred his horse through the Crow ranks. Jack leaped up behind Crazy Horse. The two warriors rode away to safety.

About noon, General Crook sent Captain Anson Mills and eight troops of cavalry down the canyon. Crook thought that Crazy Horse's village was there. Crazy Horse let the soldiers pass. He massed most of his warriors on Crook's left. Other warriors worked their way behind the soldiers. Sensing the danger, Crook sent word to Mills to return at once. Mills's cavalry appeared behind Crazy Horse's lines. The Sioux scattered and the battle was over.

Crook lost twenty-eight men and had fifty-six severely wounded. His troops had fired 25,000 rounds. Thirteen Sioux lay dead on the field.[4] A day later Crook retreated to the south. His forces remained out of action for a month. They would play no role in the coming big battle.

Crazy Horse led his warriors back to camp on the Little Bighorn. They were pleased that they had driven away Crook's forces. They mourned the dead, then they feasted and danced. Crazy Horse did not think he had won a war. Sitting Bull's vision had not yet come to pass.

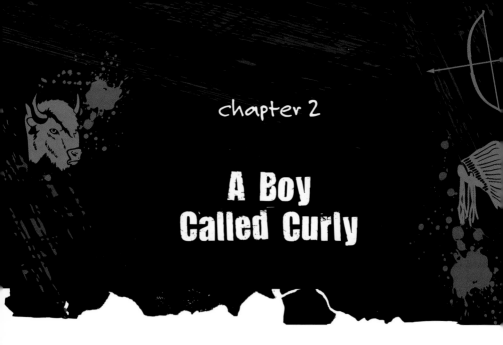

chapter 2

A Boy Called Curly

Crazy Horse was born in the fall of 1841. His birthplace lay on Rapid Creek, east of South Dakota's *Paha Sapa*—the Black Hills. His father, also called Crazy Horse, was a holy man of the Oglala Sioux. He belonged to the Hunkpatila (End of Circle) band. At tribal meetings the band always camped at one end of the crescent of tipis.

Crazy Horse's mother was a Brulé Sioux. She died when he was very young. Her younger sister took over as mother of Crazy Horse. The boy's light skin and hazel eyes set him apart. To the Sioux these features were special gifts from *Wakan Tanka* (the Great Holy). The band called him Curly. He had a sister who was two years older and a younger brother.

The Oglala were Plains Sioux. Years before, they had lived in the eastern forests of the Great Lakes. They moved west after their enemies, the Chippewas, obtained guns from white traders. The Sioux crossed the northern Great Plains in pursuit of game.

Huge herds of buffalo roamed the grasslands. In the 1700s the Sioux gained horses from the Spanish far to the south. Horses became central to their way of life. They allowed the Sioux to hunt and move from place to place more easily. Raiding other tribes for horses became a part of Oglala life.

The land where Curly grew up was harsh. Winter cold could bring death quickly. The summer sun blazed. The Oglala needed to be tough to survive. The buffalo provided most of what the Oglala needed. They used hides for robes and for

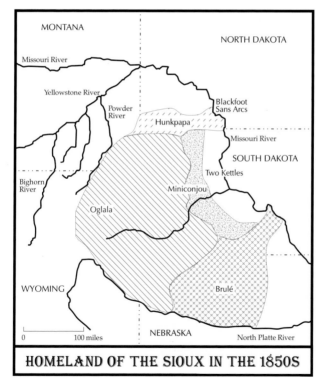

HOMELAND OF THE SIOUX IN THE 1850S

The Oglala were part of the Lakota, or western Sioux.

11

covering their tipis. They made cups and tools from the horns. They ground the hoofs to make glue. Buffalo sinews provided thread and bow strings. And sun-dried strips of buffalo meat became jerky. This food lasted a long time without spoiling. Dried meat mixed with fat and berries became pemmican, which could be stored for long periods.

From an early age Curly knew whites. The Hunkpatila leader Old Smoke liked coffee, sugar, and whiskey. He spent much time near the trading posts. Some of the travelers on the Oregon Trail thought Curly was a captured white boy. With the whites came new diseases. Many Sioux died from smallpox, influenza, and cholera.

In the summer of 1854, Curly camped with some Brulé Sioux near Fort Laramie. A cow bolted from a Mormon

The Sioux often set up their tipis in the shape of a crescent moon.

wagon train into the Brulé camp. A warrior killed the cow with an arrow. A Mormon hurried to the fort to complain. Meanwhile, the Sioux butchered the cow and ate the meat.

The army recognized Conquering Bear as leader of all the Sioux.[1] Fort commander Lieutenant Hugh Fleming sent for Conquering Bear. He demanded the return of the cow. Conquering Bear offered to let the Mormon have his pick of ponies from his herd. Fleming refused the offer.

The next morning Lieutenant John Grattan led a force of thirty-one men to the Brulé camp. Curly was with the 1,200 Sioux warriors who watched from nearby cliffs. Grattan and Conquering Bear argued for half an hour. Out of patience, Grattan ordered his men to open fire. Conquering Bear fell with nine bullet wounds. Brulé warriors poured from their tipis. Other Sioux swarmed from the cliffs. Within minutes Grattan and his men were dead. The Sioux women broke camp and headed north across the prairie.

The army took a year to exact revenge. In the summer of 1855, General William Harney led a force of 600 soldiers. On September 3, Harney found the Brulé camp. Curly was away taming a mustang. Harney attacked without mercy. The soldiers killed eighty-six Brulé, including many women and children. The soldiers mutilated their bodies. When Curly returned, he saw what no Sioux had seen before. No Sioux camp had ever been destroyed. This was a new kind of war.

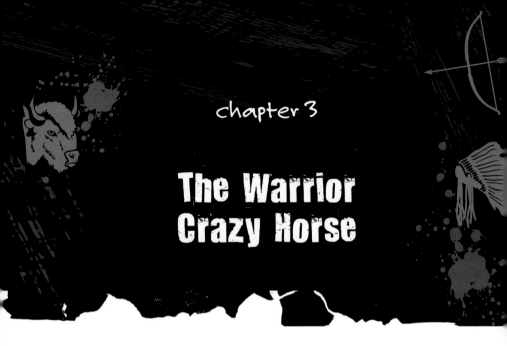

chapter 3

The Warrior Crazy Horse

Vision quests were central to the life of young Oglala men. The visions gave each person special powers. Holy men told the boys what their visions meant. The meanings were sacred. No one could change or dispute them.

When Curly was thirteen, he made his vision quest. He went into the Nebraska sand hills. There he placed sharp stones under his body to help stay awake. After three days he was about to give up. Curly stood to leave; then the vision came. A lone warrior wearing plain leggings rode from a lake. He had a small stone tied behind one ear. A zigzag of lightning was on his cheek, and spots of hail dotted his body. A red-backed hawk circled overhead.

The warrior told Curly never to wear a war bonnet. He should put dust but not paint on his war pony. Curly should rub some of the dust on his own body. He must never take anything from an enemy for himself. Then he would never be killed by an enemy. It was three years before Curly told his father about his vision. Crazy Horse told his son that the man in the vision was Curly himself. Before a battle he must dress as he saw himself in the vision. His power would be great.

When he was seventeen, Curly joined a war party. The raiders went west to Wyoming. There a scout located an Arapaho village, which had many fine horses for them to steal. The Arapaho discovered the war party's approach. They dug in behind hilltop rocks. Curly urged his horse forward. Two Arapaho charged to meet him. Curly killed them both with arrows. He leaped down from his horse. With quick strokes he removed their scalps as trophies. Then an arrow pierced his leg, and his horse ran off. He had forgotten his dream—he was taking something for himself. Curly ran downhill on foot to safety.

The Sioux held a victory dance. Curly's father walked through their camp. He sang that he was giving Curly a new name. From then on the boy would be Crazy Horse. His father would be called Worm.

Crazy Horse spent the next few years on the Powder River. With the Sioux and Cheyenne he raided against other tribes. He was a good hunter. He brought elk and buffalo meat to his family lodge. For a time Crazy Horse lived with the Cheyenne. Sometimes he lived by himself for weeks at a time. His bravery earned him respect. His friend He Dog recalled, "Crazy Horse always led his men himself when they went into battle. He always kept well in front of them."[1]

In 1862, Crazy Horse courted Red Cloud's niece Black Buffalo Woman. Red Cloud asked Crazy Horse to join him in a raid. Upon returning, Crazy Horse found Black Buffalo Woman had married No Water. Crazy Horse was angry, feeling Red Cloud had tricked him into leaving.

After winning a battle, warriors would celebrate. This painting by Frederic Remington is called *Victory Dance*.

Crazy Horse was a good hunter. He brought buffalo meat to his family lodge.

In November 1864, soldiers massacred 130 Cheyenne camped at Sand Creek, Colorado. The Cheyenne asked the Sioux to join them in the war against the whites. A new trail to the Montana goldfields crossed Sioux lands. The Sioux went to war. In early 1865, Crazy Horse took part in attacks on the Julesburg stage station. In July he acted as a decoy near the Platte Bridge station. He helped lure troopers of the Eleventh Cavalry to the spot where 1,000 warriors lay in ambush.

That summer tribal elders made Crazy Horse a "shirt wearer." He was to promote harmony, place his people before himself, and be generous. In camp he would help keep the peace. Crazy Horse received a quilled shirt made of two sheepskins. On it were 240 locks of hair. Each stood for one of his brave deeds. Crazy Horse was now a leader of his people.

chapter 4

The Fetterman Fight

I n 1862, prospectors found gold in Montana. In 1863, John Bozeman and John Jacobs blazed a new trail to the goldfields across Sioux lands. Oglala hunters brought word of the trail to Red Cloud. The threat to the Sioux hunting ground angered him. Red Cloud was determined to block the whites' use of the Bozeman Trail.

Early in 1866, the army asked Red Cloud to come to Fort Laramie. The whites offered gifts and talked of peace. The chief led 1,000 Oglala to the fort. Crazy Horse did not go with them. He said the Oglala did not need the white man's gifts. On June 13, Colonel Henry Carrington arrived with 700 soldiers. His orders were to build new forts on the Bozeman Trail. Red Cloud accused the whites of pretending to make peace while planning war.

Crazy Horse and Red Cloud watched as the soldiers built Fort Phil Kearny. They knew they couldn't destroy the forts. Instead the Sioux attacked anything outside or between the forts. On July 17, 1866, the Sioux stampeded 175 army horses and mules. From then on Fort Phil Kearny was under attack.

The siege wore on. Soldiers died when herding livestock, cutting wood, or gathering hay. Fall turned to winter. One soldier hated being on the defensive. Captain William J. Fetterman once claimed, "A single company of Regulars could whip a thousand Indians."[1] That idea cost him his life.

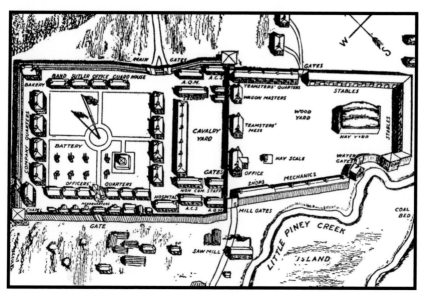

Diagram of Fort Phil Kearny. Soldiers going to the pine forests on woodcutting detail would follow the ridge immediately to the west of the fort. That way, they could avoid ambushes by Indians.

19

At dawn on December 21, the medicine man galloped into the Oglala camp. He blew shrill notes from an eagle-bone whistle. "I have a hundred dead soldiers in my hands," he cried.[2] The Sioux cheered his prophecy. The medicine man was never wrong.

Crazy Horse was the key to the Sioux battle plan. Each day a wagon train left Fort Phil Kearny to get wood. Crazy Horse was to lead a few warriors in an attack on the logging party. Soldiers would come to its rescue. The warriors would retreat slowly, wanting the soldiers to follow them. The rest of the Sioux would be lying in ambush.

Crazy Horse prepared himself with care. He applied war paint, then checked his gun and shells. He placed his bow on his back and his war club in his belt. He belted a blanket about him to ward off the cold. Crazy Horse mounted his horse. Then he led the warriors to a spot where the Powder River crossed Piney Creek.[3]

The logging party left the fort just after 10:00 A.M. An hour later Crazy Horse's men attacked the wagons. Bugles sounded in the fort. A forty-eight-man infantry company assembled. Its leader was Captain William J. Fetterman. He once boasted, "Give me eighty men and I would ride through the whole Sioux Nation."[4] Twenty-eight men of a cavalry company joined the infantry. Carrington gave Fetterman his orders. "Support the wood train. Do not engage or pursue Indians. Under no circumstances pursue over Lodge Trail Ridge."[5]

Crazy Horse decoyed a party of soldiers into an ambush outside Fort Phil Kearny. The soldiers, led by Captain William Fetterman, were wiped out to the last man.

When Fetterman's force left the fort, the decoys retreated north over Lodge Trail Ridge. Fetterman followed the warriors to the ridge top. Crazy Horse galloped close, waving his blanket. Fetterman ordered an attack. The soldiers moved north in pursuit. Ahead, 2,000 Sioux were lying in ambush.

One Sioux reported, "We held our horses' mouths so they would not neigh at the strange horses. Everything is still. The leading soldiers have reached the trail. Now they are between us."[6] Hundreds of warriors sprang from behind rocks. A cloud of arrows whistled toward the soldiers. Many were killed before they could fire a shot.

In less than an hour the last soldier was dead. Lookouts warned that more soldiers were coming from the fort. The warriors melted away. Soldiers loaded the bodies into wagons. They returned to the fort, expecting an attack. That night a blizzard brought −20°F weather. Red Cloud's forces sought the warmth of their campfires.

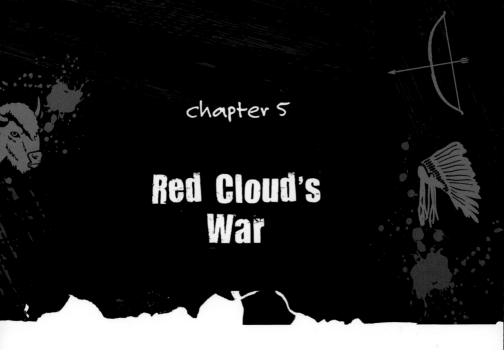

Red Cloud's War

C razy Horse's victory in the Fetterman Fight brought a quick response. The army sent a relief force to Fort Phil Kearny. Blizzards brought deep snow, so both sides waited for warmer weather. Spring came slowly to the besieged forts. In June, the soldiers received new weapons. Seven hundred fast loading Springfield rifles replaced the old muskets.

In July, 600 Cheyenne went north to attack Fort C. F. Smith. On August 1, they attacked a haymaking party. When they charged, the new rifles drove them back. Their losses in the Hayfield Fight were heavy.

The next day Red Cloud attacked near Fort Phil Kearny. Crazy Horse led a small group of warriors. They opened fire on a woodcutting party outside the fort. Crazy Horse hoped to lure away the escort party of forty soldiers. A thousand warriors lay hidden nearby. A soldier fired at Crazy Horse. The hidden Sioux streamed to the attack.

The soldiers climbed inside a ring of wagon boxes lining a corral. Crazy Horse led the Sioux circling around them.

Crazy Horse planned to charge while the soldiers reloaded after their first shots. But with the new guns the soldiers never stopped shooting. After five or six horses were hit, Crazy Horse pulled back his warriors and regrouped. He then led an attack on foot. The warriors zigzagged up a V-shaped ravine. They got within 90 yards of the soldiers. Then heavy rifle fire pinned them down.

The wagon boxes looked like pincushions filled with arrows. Crazy Horse saw the arrows could not rip through them. He led his men back down the ravine. Fire Thunder said later, "It was like green grass withering in a fire. So we picked up our people and went away. It was bad."[1] After a few hours a relief force came from the fort. The army called the battle the Wagon Box Fight.

The Model 1866 was issued to U.S. troops in 1867, and was a major factor in the Wagon Box Fight and the Hayfield Fight. The rapid rate of fire which could be achieved disrupted the tactics of attacking Sioux and Cheyenne forces. The new rifles contributed decisively to the survival and success of severely outnumbered U.S. troops.

Crazy Horse spent the rest of the winter in the Powder River country. President Andrew Johnson wanted to end the fighting on the Bozeman Trail. As a result, General William T. Sherman prepared to abandon the forts. In the summer of 1868, freighters loaded a wagon train of goods from the forts. Nearby the Sioux watched peacefully. The wagons left Fort C. F. Smith on July 29. At dawn, Crazy Horse led warriors into the fort. Carrying firebrands, they moved from building to building—setting them ablaze. Again at Fort Phil Kearny they applied their torches. Soon the forts that cost the soldiers so many lives were smoking ashes.

Red Cloud was in no hurry to sign a peace treaty. He and his warriors spent the next two months hunting. The Sioux needed a good meat supply for the coming winter. On November 4, Red Cloud appeared at Fort Laramie.

Red Cloud said that the cause of his war was now removed. He washed his hands with the dust of the floor. Then he made an X beside his name. The treaty promised that the Sioux could keep most of the Dakota Territory. The Black Hills would belong to the Sioux for as long "as the grass shall grow and the waters shall flow."[2] Whites were banned from this land forever.

Crazy Horse did not go with Red Cloud to Fort Laramie. He remained on the Powder River. He had much to celebrate. For the first time in his life he was free of whites. He could hunt and roam freely in one of the world's most beautiful regions. Wild game was plentiful.

In 1868, Red Cloud signed a peace treaty at Fort Laramie. It banned the whites from most of the Dakota Territory and promised the Sioux they could keep the land as their hunting grounds.

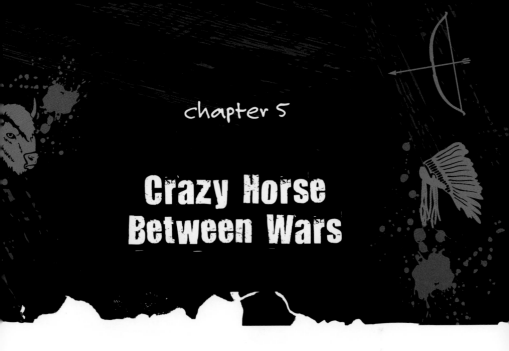

chapter 5

Crazy Horse
Between Wars

The Powder River country was at peace. In 1869, Crazy Horse led two small raids against the Crows. Most of the Sioux spent the summer hunting. They amassed a stock of buffalo robes. Crazy Horse's band headed for Fort Laramie to trade robes for weapons and supplies. When they neared the fort, soldiers fired on them. Crazy Horse had not understood the new treaty. It said the Sioux must stay on the Powder River. If they wanted to trade, they would have to move to the reservation.

In the fall of 1870, Crazy Horse led a raid on the Shoshonis. Cold rain turned to snow. Only three of their raiding party had guns. The Shoshonis outnumbered them, twelve to one. Crazy Horse thought of turning back. Hump, his oldest friend, insisted on a fight. When the Oglala attacked, the Shoshonis forced them to retreat. Crazy Horse,

At the Sun Dance, the Sioux sacrificed blood and endured pain. These were offerings for *Wakan Tanka*, the Great Holy.

Hump, and Good Weasel fought as rear guards. When Hump's horse fell, the Shoshonis killed him quickly. The others in the raiding party made it back to camp.

Crazy Horse was still in love with Black Buffalo Woman, wife of No Water. In 1871, Crazy Horse and Black Buffalo Woman rode from camp together. No Water caught up with them two days later. No Water drew a pistol and shot Crazy Horse. The bullet hit him below the left nostril, breaking his upper jaw. Crazy Horse fell forward into the fire. No Water thought he was dead. Black Buffalo Woman left with No Water. Crazy Horse slowly recovered. The elders decided Crazy Horse could no longer be a shirt wearer. He had caused trouble within the band.

The next year, Crazy Horse married Black Shawl. Within a year they had a daughter. Crazy Horse named her They Are Afraid of Her. Crazy Horse liked to gather children around him. He spent hours telling them stories. His daughter's life was cut short by cholera. Her body rested on a high scaffold in the burial ground of the Sioux. Crazy Horse mourned for three days. After that he became quiet. Crazy Horse spoke little in public.

On the Yellowstone River, surveyors plotted a route for the Northern Pacific Railroad. The army sent Lieutenant Colonel

Sitting Bull had a vision. In it, he saw soldiers falling into his camp. The Sioux fought the Battle of the Little Bighorn knowing they were going to win.

George Custer's Seventh Cavalry to guard them. Crazy Horse joined Sitting Bull in fighting the soldiers. For seven days in August 1873, the soldiers and warriors skirmished. Then each side pulled back. The surveyors and soldiers headed east. Sitting Bull and Crazy Horse spent a peaceful fall and winter on the Powder River.

Custer returned to the Black Hills in 1874. He reported rich finds of gold. Miners swarmed to *Paha Sapa*, as the Sioux called the Black Hills. In 1875, many Sioux left the reservation to join Crazy Horse. He led the warriors in attacks on the miners. But there were too many whites for him to drive out. That summer the Oglala, Hunkpapa, Sans Arcs, and Miniconjou joined with the Cheyenne. They held a great Sun Dance. Crazy Horse was present but was not a dancer. Messengers arrived, asking Crazy Horse to come to a great council. The topic would be the sale of the Black Hills. Crazy Horse refused to attend. He said, "One does not sell the earth upon which the people walk."[1]

In December, runners brought news to Crazy Horse. All Sioux were to be on their reservation by January 31, 1876. Those not there would be considered hostile. Crazy Horse refused. He led his people to join Sitting Bull. By May, lodges filled the valley of the Rosebud. In a Sun Dance, Sitting Bull offered *Wakan Tanka* 100 pieces of flesh. He saw a vision of many soldiers falling into the Sioux camp.

Every few days the camp moved to find fresh grass. In early June it moved to the valley of the Little Bighorn River.

chapter 7

At the Little Bighorn

T en thousand people camped by the Little Bighorn. They called the valley the Greasy Grass. The Cheyenne camped to the north. Below them were the lodges of the Brulé, Sans Arcs, Oglala, Blackfoot, and Miniconjou. The young warriors wanted to ride out to raid. Sitting Bull and Crazy Horse used their power to keep the tribes together. Then the tribes could defend the camp if more soldiers came. Crazy Horse knew the fight on the Rosebud was not the battle Sitting Bull saw in his vision. No soldiers had fallen into the Sioux camp.

On June 25, scouts brought word. Soldiers were coming up the Little Bighorn from the south. General Alfred Terry had ordered Custer not to attack if he found the Sioux camp. He was to wait for reinforcements. Custer disobeyed. He feared the Sioux would get away before the army could attack them. Custer divided his Seventh Cavalry into three parts. He sent Captain Frederick Benteen with 112 men to scout to the south.

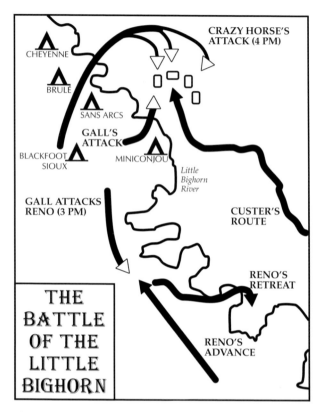

Crazy Horse led the attack on the Seventh Cavalry.

Major Marcus Reno's 150 men were to attack the camp directly. Custer would lead the remaining 215 men. He planned to swing behind the hills. Then he would attack the camp from the north. His wagon train remained far behind.

About 3:00 P.M. Reno attacked the southern edge of the Sioux camp. Short Bull's Hunkpapa warriors stopped the soldiers' charge. They killed or wounded half of Reno's men. Reno retreated across the river. Short Bull said Crazy Horse was in his lodge when Reno attacked. He and his men rode to join the fight. "Too late! You've missed the fight!" Short Bull told Crazy Horse. "Sorry to miss this fight," Crazy Horse replied. "But there's a good fight coming over the hill. That's where the big fight is going to be. We'll not miss that one."[1]

Other Oglala said Crazy Horse had helped stop Reno's charge. They said he rode with the greatest daring up and down in front of Reno's skirmish line. After the Rosebud Battle, the Sioux had picked up rifles from the dead. Many of them were jammed. "Make [the soldiers] shoot three times," Crazy Horse called out now. "Their guns will stick and you can knock them down with your clubs."[2]

The defeat of Custer and his troops at the Battle of the Little Bighorn.

More soldiers appeared on a ridge across the stream. Gall led the Hunkpapa in a counterattack across the Little Bighorn. Sitting Bull feared the soldiers would charge. The Sioux might then break and run. Instead the soldiers dismounted. The soldiers pulled back toward the top of a hill. Soon the battlefield faded into a cloud of dust. Crazy Horse knew how the battle would turn out. Sitting Bull's vision had told him. Crazy Horse led the Oglala and in a circling movement. They swept in on Custer's men from the north. The Sioux were on all sides of the soldiers.

Crazy Horse waved his rifle and swung his war club. One warrior later said, "Crazy Horse was the bravest man I ever saw. He rode closest to the soldiers, yelling to his warriors. All the soldiers were shooting at him, but he was never hit."[3]

Crazy Horse and his men charged into Custer's ranks. Their battle cries filled the air. They killed the soldiers with their arrows, clubs, guns, and lances. Not one soldier remained alive. The Sioux stripped the soldiers' bodies of clothes, ammunition, and weapons. They took the army saddles and horses.[4] Then they returned to besiege Reno. Their attack was half-hearted, since they had done enough that day.

In this battle Crazy Horse was decisive. His courage was an example for other warriors. His attack from the north made Custer's defeat sure. At the Little Bighorn, Custer was not only outnumbered. He was out-generaled.[5]

chapter 8

Crazy Horse Surrenders

The next day scouts warned that more soldiers were coming. The Sioux split into groups. Sitting Bull led the Hunkpapa southwest. But Crazy Horse led the Oglala southeast. Many Oglala returned to the reservation. Soon Crazy Horse led fewer than 600 warriors.[1]

The army had lost a battle, not a war. Congress voted to send 2,500 new soldiers to Generals Terry and Crook. The generals waited for reinforcements. Crook remained on the Powder River. Terry camped on the Yellowstone.

In August, Crazy Horse attacked miners in the Black Hills. His attacks were small scale. Sometimes Crazy Horse raided on his own. He Dog tried to stop him. "My friend, you are past the foolish years of the wild young warrior. You belong to the people now. [You] must think of them."[2]

That month Congress passed a new law. It ordered the Sioux to sign over the Black Hills, Powder River, and

Bighorn country. The Sioux would have to move to a reservation on the Missouri River or to Oklahoma. They would get no provisions until they agreed. Red Cloud and Spotted Tail signed the treaty.

On September 9, Captain Anson Mills led 150 soldiers in an attack on a Brulé village. Runners took word to Crazy Horse. He led 200 warriors to the rescue. Mills held his ground. That afternoon Crook arrived with 1,850 more soldiers. Crazy Horse pulled back. Crook burned the village, then marched to Deadwood to resupply.

Crook planned a winter campaign. In November, his force found a Cheyenne camp. In a surprise attack they killed forty Cheyenne. Freezing weather killed many more. The Cheyenne marched north through the snow for two weeks. Crazy Horse and the Oglala took them in and shared the little food and supplies they had.

A few weeks later, General Nelson Miles sent a scout to Crazy Horse. Miles asked Crazy Horse to surrender. Hunting was bad, and food was short. Crazy Horse was tired of fighting. His small band could not hold out forever.[3] He agreed to surrender. He sent eight subchiefs to talk about terms. When the subchiefs neared the army camp, Miles's Crow scouts attacked, killing five of them. That ended Miles's hopes for Crazy Horse's surrender.

Miles's troops found Crazy Horse's camp on January 1. Crazy Horse fought a rear guard action as his people fled.

36

The fighting lasted a week. Then Miles returned to his base. Crazy Horse found a small herd of buffalo. It provided food for the Oglala. Sitting Bull urged Crazy Horse to join him in a move to Canada.[4] Crazy Horse refused. He thought he would be for the rest of the winter.

In February, Crook sent a message to Crazy Horse. He asked Crazy Horse to surrender at Fort Robinson, Nebraska. Crook promised he could have his own agency in the Powder River country. Crazy Horse sent word he would come when the weather was better.

Crazy Horse arrived May 6, 1877. Twenty thousand watched him march in. The parade of 800 Oglala and 1,700

Crazy Horse and his band of Indians marched from Camp Sheridan to surrender to General Crook at the Red Cloud Agency.

ponies was two miles long. Crazy Horse surrendered to Lieutenant William Clark. The warrior extended his left hand. Crazy Horse explained, "*Kola* [friend], I shake with this hand because my heart is on this side. I want this peace to last forever."[5]

Crook delayed setting up an agency for Crazy Horse. Crook asked Crazy Horse to travel to Washington, D.C. Crazy Horse said he did not want to meet the *Great Father* (President of the United States). Crook asked Crazy Horse to join him in chasing Chief Joseph and the Nez Percé. Again Crazy Horse refused. He said he had come to the agency for peace, not war. Other Sioux chiefs became jealous of Crazy Horse. They told Crook that Crazy Horse was planning to kill him and escape to Canada.

chapter 9

The Killing of Crazy Horse

The whites panicked. They believed the rumors that Crazy Horse planned to go to war again. General Crook arrived at Fort Robinson on September 2. He ordered the Sioux to move to the base of a nearby mesa. Here he would hold a council. Most of the Sioux packed up and went. Crazy Horse refused to go.

Two days later the army came to arrest Crazy Horse. Four hundred warriors rode with eight companies of the Third Cavalry. Crazy Horse and Black Shawl fled before they arrived. Lieutenant Clark offered $200 for Crazy Horse's capture.

Crazy Horse reached the Spotted Tail Agency the evening of September 5. His uncle, Spotted Tail, told Crazy Horse, "I am chief here. We keep the peace. You say you want to come to this agency to live peaceably. If you stay here, you must listen to me. That is all!"[1]

Crazy Horse promised his uncle he would obey him and live there in peace. Crazy Horse said he had not threatened to go to war again. He did not plan to kill General Crook. Lieutenant Jesse Lee was the agent at Spotted Tail Agency. Crazy Horse promised him that he would ride back to Fort Robinson the next day and explain. Lee promised he would talk with the fort commander there.

On September 6, 1877, Spotted Tail and Touch the Clouds rode beside Crazy Horse on the forty-five mile ride back. He Dog rode up to Crazy Horse. "Watch your step—you are going into a bad place," he warned.

The fort commander, Lieutenant Colonel Luther Bradley had his orders. He was to arrest Crazy Horse and confine him. Captain James Kennington led Crazy Horse toward the guardhouse. Crazy Horse still believed agent Lee's promise. He thought he was going to speak to the fort commander.

Little Big Man, Turning Bear, Leaper, and Wooden Sword surrounded Crazy Horse. Crazy Horse stepped into the guardhouse. He saw the small barred windows of a cell. He whipped about, drawing his knife. Little Big Man held his friend's arms. Private William Gentles stabbed him in the back with his bayonet. A second stab pierced his kidneys. He fell into Little Big Man's arms. Crazy Horse said softly, "Let me go, my friends. You have got me hurt enough."

Carving of the Crazy Horse monument on Thunderbird Mountain, North Dakota, began in 1948.

Crazy Horse died an hour later. He was only thirty-six years old. His father placed his body on a platform at the Spotted Trail Agency. Later he wrapped the bones in a buffalo robe. He hid them in a place only he knew. It was somewhere near Wounded Knee Creek, South Dakota.

Six generations later over 50,000 Sioux live in North and South Dakota.[2] The Oglala live on Pine Ridge Reservation. They continue to honor and remember Crazy Horse. In 1990 a British magazine posed a question: Little Bighorn was the Plains tribes' finest hour. Why was there no monument to Crazy Horse there?[3] One answer lies two hundred miles farther east. Sculptor Korczak Ziolkowski planned to create a giant figure of Crazy Horse astride a war pony. He began to carve the monument from Thunderbird Mountain in the Black Hills. The sculpture would be 563 feet high and 641 feet long. Crazy Horse's head would be over 87 feet tall; his pony's, 219 feet.[4]

Not all Native Americans looked on the statue the same way. Chief Henry Standing Bear said, "Please carve us a mountain so the white man will know that the red man had heroes too."

Sioux medicine man Lame Deer disagreed. "The whole idea of making a beautiful wild mountain into a statue of [Crazy Horse] is a pollution of the landscape."

Fools Crow added, "This mountain doesn't want the statue to be built. The ghost of Crazy Horse doesn't want it. It will never be finished."[5]

Chapter Notes

Chapter 1
1. Benjamin Capps, *The Great Chiefs* (New York: Time Life, 1975), p. 154.
2. Dorothy M. Johnson, *Warrior for a Lost Nation* (Philadelphia: The Westminster Press, 1966), p. 72.
3. Stephen E. Ambrose, *Crazy Horse and Custer* (Garden City, N.Y.: Doubleday & Co., 1975), p. 388.
4. Capps, p. 157.

Chapter 2
1. Stephen E. Ambrose, *Crazy Horse and Custer* (Garden City, N.Y.: Doubleday & Co., 1975), p. 50.

Chapter 3
1. Jason Hook, *American Indian Warrior Chiefs* (Poole, Dorset, U.K.: Firebird Books, 1989), p. 72.

Chapter 4
1. Alexander Adams, *Sitting Bull* (New York: G.P. Putnam's Sons, 1974), p. 133.
2. Paul and Dorothy Goble, *Brave Eagle's Account of the Fetterman Fight* (New York: Pantheon Books, 1972), p. 41.
3. Mari Sandoz, *Crazy Horse* (New York: Hastings House, 1942), p. 198.
4. Ralph K. Andrist, *The Long Death: The Last Days of the Plains Indians* (New York: Macmillan, 1964), p. 108.
5. Ibid., p. 113.
6. Goble, p. 48.

Chapter 5
1. John Niehardt, *Black Elk Speaks* (Lincoln, Neb.: University of Nebraska Press, 1961), p. 17.
2. Sheila Black, *Sitting Bull and the Battle of Little Big Horn* (Englewood Cliffs, N.J.: Silver Burdett, 1989), p. 71.

Chapter 6
1. Jason Hook, *American Indian Warrior Chiefs* (Poole, Dorset, U.K.: Firebird Books, 1989), p. 83.

Chapter 7
1. Stephen E. Ambrose, *Crazy Horse and Custer* (Garden City, N.Y.: Doubleday & Co., 1975), p. 403.
2. Mari Sandoz, *Crazy Horse* (New York: Hastings House, 1942), p. 326.
3. W. A. Graham, *The Custer Myth* (Harrisburg, Pa.: Stackpole, 1953), p. 110.
4. Shannon Garst, *Crazy Horse: Great Warrior of the Sioux* (Boston: Houghton Mifflin, 1950), p. 131.
5. Ambrose, p. 411.

Chapter 8
1. Stephen E. Ambrose, *Crazy Horse and Custer* (Garden City, N.Y.: Doubleday & Co., 1975), p. 416.
2. Mari Sandoz, *Crazy Horse* (New York: Hastings House, 1942), p. 337.
3. Bill and Jan Moeller, *Crazy Horse: His Life, His Lands* (Wilsonville, Ore.: Beautiful America, 1987), p. 112.
4. Ambrose, p. 421.
5. Moeller, p. 115.

Chapter 9
1. Stephen E. Ambrose, *Crazy Horse and Custer* (Garden City, N.Y.: Doubleday & Co., 1975), p. 432.
2. *The World Almanac and Book of Facts 1993* (New York: Pharos Books, 1993), p. 459.
3. *The Economist*, Sept. 8, 1990, p. 26.
4. *American Heritage*, June 1977, p. 25.
5. Ibid.

Glossary

band—A subdivision of a tribe, sometimes only a few dozen in number.

chief—A leader of a band or tribe; often a chief was limited to a specific role, such as leadership in war.

council—A meeting of the adults in a tribe; all warriors had the right to express their opinions.

medicine man—A Native American priest. Medicine men often combined telling the future and practicing medicine.

pemmican—A food prepared by mixing dried meat with fat and berries. Pemmican could be stored for long periods of time.

reservation—An area set aside by the government to be the permanent home of a group of Native Americans.

scouts—Skilled frontiersmen; scouts served as lookouts, read tracks, found trails, and located game.

Sun Dance—A religious ceremony practiced by a number of Native American peoples, primarily those of the Plains Nations. The dance thanked the Great Spirit for past favors and insured a favorable future.

treaty—An agreement between two governments; treaties between Native Americans and whites often dealt with sale of land.

tribe—A large group of Native Americans, speaking a common language and living in the same area.

vision quest—A journey made by young Sioux deprived themselves of sleep and food. When exhausted, they fell asleep and dreamed. They believed the gods spoke to them in their dreams.

warrior—A Native American fighting man.

Further Reading

Books

Brimner, Larry Dane. *Chief Crazy Horse: Following a Vision.* New York: Marshall Cavendish Benchmark, 2009.

Freedman, Rusell. *The Life and Death of Crazy Horse.* New York: Holiday House, 1996.

Haugen, Brenda. *Crazy Horse: Sioux Warrior.* Minneapolis, Minn.: Compass Point Books, 2006.

Rice, Earle, Jr. *The Brothers Custer: Galloping to Glory.* Hockessin, DE: Mitchell Lane Publishers, 2008.

Walker, Paul Robert. *Remember Little Bighorn: Indians, Soldiers, and Scouts Tell Their Stories.* Washington, DC: National Geographic Children's Books, 2006.

Internet Addresses

Crazy Horse—History.com Articles, Video, Pictures and Facts
<http://www.history.com/topics/crazy-horse>

Legends of America: Battles and Massacres of the Indian Wars in the American West
<http://www.legendsofamerica.com/na-indianwarbattles-1.html>

PBS: New Perspectives on the West—Crazy Horse
<http://www.pbs.org/weta/thewest/people/a_c/crazyhorse.htm>

Index

A

Arapaho, 15

B

Benteen, Capt. Frederick, 31–32
Black Buffalo Woman, 16, 28
Black Shawl, 29, 39
Bozeman, John, 18
Bozeman Trail, 18, 25
Bradley, Lt. Col. Luther, 40
Brulé, 10, 11, 12, 13, 31

C

Carrington, Col. Henry, 18, 20
Cheyenne, 15, 17, 23, 24, 30, 31, 34, 36
Chief Joseph, 38
Chippewas, 10
Clark, Lt. William, 38
Conquering Bear, 13
Crazy Horse
   birth and childhood, 10–13
   and Black Hills miners, 30, 35
   burns Bozeman Trail forts, 25
   and Custer on Yellowstone, 29–30
   death and burial, 40, 42
   in Fetterman Fight, 20–22, 23
   in Hayfield Fight, 23, 24
   legacy, 41, 42
   at Little Bighorn, 31–34
   marries Black Shawl, 29
   on Powder River, 15, 20, 25–26,
   27–29
   refuses to go on reservation, 5, 27, 35,
   36–37
   at Rosebud Creek, 5–9, 30, 31
   as shirt wearer, 17, 28
   at Spotted Tail Agency, 39–40, 42
   surrenders, 36–37
   territory of, 7
   on vision quest, 14–15
   in Wagon Box Fight, 23–25
Crook, Gen. George, 5, 8, 9, 35, 36, 37,
   38, 39, 40
Crows, 8, 9, 27, 26
Custer, Lt. Col. George, 7, 29–30, 31–32,
   33, 34

F

Fetterman, Capt. William, 7, 19, 20–22
Fire Thunder, 24–25
Fleming, Lt. Hugh, 13
Fools Crow, 42
Fort C. F. Smith, 7, 23, 25
Fort Laramie, 7, 18, 25, 26, 27
Fort Phil Kearny, 7, 19–22, 23, 25
Fort Robinson, 39, 40

G

Gall, 32, 34
Gentles, Priv. William, 40
Good Weasel, 28
Grattan, Lt. John, 13

H

Harney, Gen. William, 13
He Dog, 15, 35, 40
Hump, 27–28
Hunkpapa, 11, 30, 32, 34, 35
Hunkpatila, 10, 12

J

Jacobs, John, 18
Johnson, Pres. Andrew, 25

K

Kennington, Capt. James, 40

L

Lame Deer, 42
Leaper, 40
Lee, Lt. Jesse, 40
Little Bighorn, Battle of, 29, 32–34, 42
Little Bighorn River, 30, 31, 32
Little Big Man, 40

M

Miles, Nelson, 36–37
Mills, Anson, 9, 36
Miniconjou, 11, 30, 31

N

No Water, 16, 28

O

Old Smoke, 12

P

Pine Ridge Reservation, 42

R

Red Cloud, 9, 16, 18, 19, 22, 23, 25, 26, 36
Red Cloud, Jack, 9
Red Cloud Agency, 37
Reno, Maj. Marcus, 32–33, 34
Rosebud Creek, 5–9, 30, 31, 33

S

Sand Creek, 17
Sans Arcs, 11, 30, 31
Seventh Cavalry, 30, 31–34
Sherman, Gen. William T., 25
Short Bull, 32, 33
Shoshonis, 8, 27, 28
Sitting Bull, 5, 9, 29, 30, 35, 37
Spotted Tail, 36, 39, 401
Spotted Tail Agency, 39, 40
Standing Bear, Chief Henry, 42
Sun Dance, 5, 28, 30

T

Terry, Gen. Alfred, 31, 35
Thunderbird Mountain, 41, 42
Touch the Clouds, 40
Turning Bear, 40

W

Wakan Tanka (the Great Holy), 5, 10, 28, 30
Wooden Sword, 40
Worm (Crazy Horse's father), 10, 15, 42

Z

Ziolkowski, Korczak, 42